WORCESTERSHIRE
Wit & Humour

LEIGH ELGAR

BRADWELL
BOOKS

Published by Bradwell Books
9 Orgreave Close Sheffield S13 9NP
Email: books@bradwellbooks.co.uk
Compiled by Leigh Elgar

All rights reserved. No part of this publication may be reproduced, stored in a retrieval system or transmitted in any form or by any means, electronic, mechanical, photocopying, recording or otherwise without the prior permission of Bradwell Books.

British Library Cataloguing in Publication Data: a catalogue record for this book is available from the British Library.

1st Edition

ISBN: 9781910551080

Print: Gomer Press, Llandysul, Ceredigion SA44 4JL
Design by: jenksdesign@yahoo.co.uk/07506 471162
Illustrations: ©Tim O'Brien 2014

Two elderly ladies in Malvern had been friends for many decades. Over the years, they had shared all kinds of fun but of late their activities had been limited to meeting a few times a week to play cards. One day, they were playing pontoon when one looked at the other and said, "Now don't get mad at me, my dear. I know we've been friends for a long time but I just can't think of your name. I've thought and thought, but I can't remember it. Please tell me what your name is." Her friend got a bit cross and, for ages, she just sat and glared at her. Finally she said, "How soon do you need to know?"

How do you get a sweet old Worcestershire granny to swear? Get another sweet old Worcestershire granny to shout "BINGO!"

A teacher at a school in Kidderminster was having a little trouble getting her Year 11 pupils to understand grammar. "These are what we call the pronouns," she said, "we use them with verbs like this: I am, you are, he/she is." The pupils looked at her with glazed expressions.

Trying a different tack, she said, "Lauren, give me a sentence with the pronoun, 'I' in it."

Lauren began, "I is..."

"No, no, no, no, no NO, NO!" shouted the teacher, "Never, 'I is', always, 'I am'... now try again."

Lauren looked puzzled and a little hurt, thought a while then began again more quietly, "I... am...the ninth letter of the alphabet."

WORCESTERSHIRE Wit & Humour

The magistrate at Worcester County Court spoke sharply to the defendant, "But if you saw the lady driving towards you, why didn't you give her half the road?"

"I was going to, your Honour," replied the motorist, "…as soon as I could work out which half she wanted."

Man: "My poor wife had to go and see a doctor when we were in Worcestershire."
Friend: "Redditch?"
Man: "Yes but she would keep scratching it."

Two rival cricketers from Ombersley and Eckington were having a chat.

"The local team wants me to play for them very badly," said the man from Ombersley.

"Well," said his friend, "you're just the man for the job."

Fred's wife has been missing for over a week. The police liaison officer warned him to prepare for the worst…so Fred went to the charity shop to get all her clothes back.

Simon was down on his luck so he thought he would try getting a few odd jobs by calling at the posh houses in Broadway. After a few "no chances", a guy in one of the big houses thought he would give him a break and says, "The porch needs painting so I'll give you £50 to paint it for me."

"You're life-saver, mister," says Simon, "I'll get started right away!" Time passes until…

"There you go, I'm all done with the painting."

"Well, here's your £50," says the homeowner, handing over some crisp tenners.

"Thanks very much," says Simon, pocketing the money, "Oh and by the way, it's a Ferrari, not a Porsche!"

WORCESTERSHIRE Wit & Humour

Two elderly ladies were enjoying a small sherry in their local in Clifton Upon Teme.

One said to the other, "Was it love at first sight when you met your late husband?"

"No, I don't think so," came the reply, "I didn't know how much money he had when I first met him!"

A lad from Redditch was bragging to his mate: "My computer beat me at chess, but it were no match for me at kick boxing."

Just before the Novices' Chase at Worcester racecourse, the trainer was giving last minute instructions to the jockey and appeared to slip something into the horse's mouth just as a steward walked by.

"What was that?" inquired the steward.

"Oh nothing," said the trainer, "just a polo."

He offered one to the steward and had one himself. After the suspicious steward had left the scene, the trainer continued with his instructions.

"Just keep on the rail. You're on a dead cert. The only thing that could possibly pass you down the home straight is either the steward or me."

In the village of Upton Warren a couple are bickering…

Wife: "I'm telling you, there's trouble with the car. It has water in the injectors."

Husband: "Water in the injectors? That's ridiculous."

Wife: "I tell you the car has water in the injectors."

Husband: "You don't even know what injectors are. I'll check it out. Where's the car?"

Wife: "In Settling Pond."

WORCESTERSHIRE Wit & Humour

A Kidderminster Harriers fan was watching his team play in a packed Aggborough stadium. There was only one empty seat - right next to him.

"Who does that seat belong to?" asked Dave from the row behind.

"I got the ticket for my wife." replied the Harriers fan.
"But why isn't she here?"

"I'm afraid she died in a tragic accident."
"So you're keeping the seat vacant as a mark of respect." said Dave.

"No," said the Harriers fan, "I offered it to all of my friends."

"Then why didn't they take it?" asked a puzzled Dave.

"They've all gone to the funeral."

A lad from Worcester who had just started his first term at Shrewsbury School asked a prefect, "Can you tell me where the library's at?"

The older student said disdainfully, "At Shrewsbury School we never end a sentence with a preposition."

The new boy tried again, "Can you tell me where the library's at, you wally?"

Derek and Duncan were long-time neighbours in Bromsgrove. Every time, Derek saw Duncan coming round to his house, his heart sank. This was because he knew that, as always, Duncan would be visiting him in order to borrow something and he was fed up with it.

"I'm not going to let Duncan get away with it this time," he said quietly to his wife, "watch what I'm about to do."

"Hi there, I wondered if you were thinking about using your hedge trimmer this afternoon?" asked Duncan.

"Oh, I'm very sorry," said Derek, trying to look apologetic, "but I'm actually going to be using it all afternoon."

"In that case," replied Duncan with a big grin, "you won't be using your golf clubs, will you? Mind if I borrow them?"

WORCESTERSHIRE Wit & Humour

A lawyer from Shrewsbury and a businessman from Worcester ended up sitting next to each other on a long-haul flight.

The lawyer started thinking that he could have some fun at the man from Worcester's expense and asked him if he'd like to play a fun game. The businessman was tired and just wanted to relax. He politely declined the offer and tried to sleep. The lawyer persisted, explaining, "I ask you a question, and if you don't know the answer, you pay me just £5; you ask me one, and if I don't know the answer, I will pay you £500."

This got the businessman a little more interested and he finally agreed to play the game.

WORCESTERSHIRE Wit & Humour

The lawyer asked the first question, "What's the distance from the Earth to the moon?"

The man from Worcester said nothing, but reached into his pocket, pulled out a five-pound note and handed it to the lawyer.

Now, it was his turn to ask a question. He asked the lawyer, "What goes up a hill with three legs, and comes down with four?"

The lawyer scratched his head. He looked the question up on his laptop and searched the web. He sent emails to his most well-read friends. He used the air-phone to call his colleagues in Shrewsbury, but he still came up with nothing. After hours of searching, he finally gave up.

He woke up the businessman and handed him £500. The man pocketed the cash smugly and dozed off again.

The lawyer was wild with curiosity and wanted to know the answer. He shook the businessman awake. "Well? What goes up a hill with three legs and comes down with four?" he demanded.

The businessman reached into his pocket, handed the lawyer £5 and went straight back to sleep.

An elderly couple from Kidderminster are sitting at the dining table in their semi-detached house talking about making preparations for writing their wills. Bill says to his missus, Edna, "I've been thinking my dear, if I go first to meet me maker I don't want you to be on your own for too long. In fact, I think you could do worse than marry Colin in the Chemists or Dave with the fruit stall in the market. They'd provide for you and look after you when I'm gone."

"That's very kind on you to think about me like that, Bill," replied Edna, "but I've already made my own arrangements!"

WORCESTERSHIRE Wit & Humour

A bloke from Droitwich goes into an artist's studio and asks if the artist could paint a picture of him surrounded by beautiful, scantily clad women. The artist agrees but he is intrigued by this strange request. He asks his new client why he wants such a picture painted and the bloke says, "Well, if I die before me missus when she finds this painting she'll wonder which one I spent all me money on!"

The next day the bloke's wife goes into the artist's studio and asks him to paint her wearing a big diamond necklace and matching earrings.

"Of course, madam," says the artist, "but may I ask why?"

"Well," replies the woman, "if I die before me husband I want his new woman to be frantic searching for all me jewellery!"

WORCESTERSHIRE Wit & Humour

A Worcestershire man is driving through Shropshire when he passes a farmer standing in the middle of a huge field. He pulls the car over and watches the farmer standing stock-still, doing absolutely nothing. Intrigued, the man walks over to the farmer and asks him, "Excuse me sir, but what are you doing?"

The farmer replies, "I'm trying to win a Nobel Prize."

"How?" Asks the puzzled Worcestershire man.

"Well," says the farmer, "I heard they give the prize to people who are outstanding in their field."

WORCESTERSHIRE Wit & Humour

A well-known academic from the Shrewsbury School was giving a lecture on the philosophy of language to sixth-formers at Malvern College. He came to a curious aspect of English grammar.

"You will note," said the somewhat stuffy scholar, "that in the English language, two negatives can mean a positive, but it is never the case that two positives can mean a negative."

To which someone at the back responded, "Yeah, yeah."

Q: What did one ocean say to the other ocean?
A: Nothing, they just waved.

A police officer was patrolling the lanes outside Stourport-on-Severn one night, when he noticed a car swerving all over the road. Quickly, he turned on his lights and siren and pulled the driver over. "Sir, do you know you're all over the road? Please step out of the car."

When the man got out of the car, the policeman told him to walk in a straight line.

"I'd be happy to, offisher," said the drunk, "if you can just get the line to stop moving about."

Q: What's the difference between a new husband and a new dog?
A: After a year, the dog is still excited to see you.

A lady works in Worcester and everyday she walks past a pet shop there. One day she notices a parrot in the window and stops to admire the bird. The parrot says to her, "Ay, wench, you're a right slummocking cow."

Well, the lady is furious! She storms off but, on her way back from work, she passes the same parrot and, when it sees her, the bird says, "Ay, wench, you're a right slummocking cow."

She is incredibly angry now so she goes to the manager and threatens to sue the pet shop. She demands to have the bird put down. The manager apologises profusely and promises that the bird won't say it again. The next day, she decides to go back and check. She walks past the parrot and, when it sees her, it says, "Ay, wench."

The woman stops, scowls and with an icy stare, says, "Yes?"

The parrot struts back and forth on its perch in a cocky manner gawping at her, then it says, "You know."

A man from Powick said to his wife, "Get your coat on, love. I'm off to the club."

His wife said, "That's nice. You haven't taken me out for years."

He said, "You're not coming with me...I'm turning the heating off when I go out."

At a cricket match in Cookley, a fast bowler sent one down and it just clipped the bail. As nobody yelled "Ow's att!" the batsman picked up the bail and replaced it. He looked at the umpire and said, "Windy today isn't it?"

"Yes," said the umpire, "mind it doesn't blow your cap off when you're walking back to the pavilion."

A DEFRA Inspector goes to a small farm near Hallow and knocks the door of the humble, tied cottage. A young boy opens the door and asks what business the man has on his parent's property.

"I've come to inspect the farm for compliance with EU regulations, my boy. Where's your father?"

"You can't speak to him, he's busy," says the surly child.

"I shall speak to him. He's had notice of my visit." the Inspector retorted firmly.

"Well, he's feeding the pigs at the moment," says the boy, "you'll be able to tell me father easy enough - he's the one wearing a hat!"

One freezing cold December day, two blondes went for a walk in the Wyre Forest in search of the perfect Christmas tree. Finally, after five hours looking, one turns to the other and says crossly, "That's it, I've had enough. I'm chopping down the next fir tree we see, whether it's decorated or not!"

A policeman stops a drunk wandering the streets of Redditch at four in the morning and says, "Can you explain why you are out at this hour, sir?"

The drunk replies, "If I was able to explain myself, I would have been home with the wife ages ago."

What do you get if you cross Telford United F.C. with an OXO cube?
A laughing stock.

Four fonts walk into a bar. The barman says, "Oi - get out! We don't want your type in here."

A reporter from The Worcester News was covering the local football league and went to see Arrow Valley F.C. versus Stoke Sporting Reserves. One of the Arrow Valley players looked so old, he went over to him and said, "You know you might be the oldest man playing in the league. How do you do it at your age?"

The man replied, "I drink eight pints of cider every night, smoke two packets of fags a day, and eat loads of bacon cobs."

"Wow, that is incredible!" said the reporter, "How old did you say you were?"

"Twenty-two." said the player proudly.

A Bewdley couple, Enid and Sidney, are having matrimonial difficulties and seek the advice of a counsellor. The couple are shown into a room where the counsellor asks Enid what problems, in her opinion, she faces in her relationship with Sidney.

"Well," she starts, "he shows me no affection, I don't seem to be important to him anymore. We don't share the same interests and I don't think he loves me at all." Enid has tears in her eyes as the counsellor walks over to her, gives her a big hug and kisses her firmly on the lips.

Sidney looks on in passive disbelief. The counsellor turns to Sidney and says, "This is what Enid needs once a day for the next month. Can you see that she gets it?"

Sidney looks unsettled, "Well I can drop her off everyday other than Wednesdays when I play snooker and Sundays when I go fishing!"

Q: What's an Evesham man's idea of a balanced diet?
A: A pint of larger in each hand.

Over a candlelit dinner in Evesham Susan's boyfriend, a Shropshire lad, proposed marriage to her. "I love the simple things in life," she said with a smile, "but I don't want one of them for my husband."

The Worcester Hockey Club is having a bad season. One day the team coach has an idea to advertise for a star player, so he places an ad in the Worcester News.

A few weeks go by and no replies. Then one wet afternoon there's a knock on the clubhouse door. In walks this horse and says, "Hello, coach, I see you're after a new hockey player?"

"Yes." says the surprised coach.

"I'm very good, great ball control, and superb passing skills. All in all, I'm a brilliant team player." says the horse.

"Is that so?" says the coach, thinking here's nothing in the rules that says a horse can't play for the team and he can't be any worst than some of the current players. "You're hired, and you play this weekend."

So, the day arrives and the Worcester Hockey Club line up for their first game with a horse at centre-half. The game starts slowly and the horse doesn't move much, but when he gets the ball he's able to go round people and change the game. Eventually, the horse gets the ball on the half-way line, tries his luck and scores.

After the game the horse was relaxing with a nice G&T in the bar and a team-mate came up to congratulate him on winning the game for the team.

"But why don't you run?" asked the player
"RUN!" Thundered the horse, "RUN! My dear chap, if I could run I'd be going over the jumps at Worcester racecourse!"

A police officer arrived at the scene of a major pile up on the M5.

The officer runs over to the front car and asks the driver, "Are you seriously hurt?"

The driver turns to the officer and says, "How the heck should I know? Do I look like a lawyer?"

A man went to the doctor and said, "I've just been playing rugby for the Worcester Warriors and I felt fine but I got back home and I found that when I touched my legs, my arms, my head, and everywhere else, it really hurt."

After a thorough examination the doctor said, "You've broken your finger."

A policeman stops a man in a car in the middle of Bromsgrove with a sheep in the front seat.

"Ay, what are you doing with that sheep?" He asks. "You should take it to a zoo."

The following week, the same policeman sees the same man again with the sheep in the front seat of the car. Both of them are wearing sunglasses. The policeman pulls him over. "I thought you were going to take that sheep to the zoo?"

The man replies, "I did. We had such a good time we are going to the coast this weekend!"

One night an old couple in Upton-Upon-Severn were lying in bed. The husband was falling asleep but the wife was in a romantic mood and wanted to talk.

She said, "You used to hold my hand when we were courting, my dear."

Wearily he reached across, held her hand for a second and tried to get back to sleep.

A few moments later she said, "Then you used to kiss me, my dear."

Mildly irritated, he reached across, gave her a peck on the cheek and settled down to sleep.

Thirty seconds later she said, "Then you used to nibble my neck, my dear."

Angrily, he threw back the bedclothes and got out of bed.
"Where are you going?" she asked.

"To get me teeth!"

Three old boys, all a bit hard of hearing, were playing golf one fine day at the Worcestershire Golf Club.
One remarked to the other, "Windy, isn't it?"
"No," the second man replied, "it's Thursday."
"So am I," chimed in the third man, "let's have a beer."

A bloke walked up to the foreman of a road laying gang in Evesham and asked for a job. "I haven't got one for you today." said the foreman, looking up from his newspaper. "But if you walk half a mile down there, you'll find the gang and you can see if you like the work. I can put you on the list for tomorrow." "That's great, mate," said the bloke as he wandered off down the road.

At the end of the shift, the man walked past the foreman and shouted, "Thanks, mate. See you in the morning."

The foreman looked up from his paper and called back, "You've enjoyed yourself then?"

"Yes, I have!" the bloke shouted, "But can I have a shovel or a pick to lean on like the rest of the gang tomorrow?"

WORCESTERSHIRE Wit & Humour

Sam worked in a telephone marketing company in Worcester. One day he walked into his boss's office and said, "I'll be honest with you, I know the economy isn't great, but I have three companies after me, and, with respect, I would like to ask for a pay rise."

After a few minutes of haggling, his manager finally agreed to a 5% pay rise, and Sam happily got up to leave.

"By the way," asked the boss as Sam went to the door, "which three companies are after you?"

"The electric company, the water company, and the phone company." Sam replied.

WORCESTERSHIRE Wit & Humour

A farmer was driving along a country road near the village of Ab Lench with a large load of fertiliser. A little boy, playing in front of his cottage, saw him and called out, "What do you have on your truck?"

"Fertiliser," the farmer replied.

"What are you going to do with it?" asked the little boy. "Put it on strawberries," answered the farmer.

"You ought to live here," the little boy advised him. "we put sugar and cream on ours."

WORCESTERSHIRE Wit & Humour

It was a quiet night in Pershore and a man and his wife were fast asleep, when there was an unexpected knock on the door. The man looked at his alarm clock. It was half past three in the morning. "I'm not getting out of bed at this time," he thought and rolled over.

There was another louder knock.

"Aren't you going to answer that?" asked his wife irritably.

So the man dragged himself out of bed and went downstairs. He opened the door to find a strange man standing outside. It didn't take the homeowner long to realise the man was drunk. "Hi there," slurred the stranger. "can you give me a push?" "No, I'm sorry I most certainly can't. It's half past three in the morning and I was in bed." said the man and he slammed the front door.

He went back up to bed and told his wife what happened.

"That wasn't very nice of you," she said. "remember that night we broke down in the pouring rain on the way to pick the kids up from the babysitter, and you had to knock on that man's door to get us started again? What would have happened if he'd told us to get lost?"

"But the man who just knocked on our door was absolutely puddled." replied her husband.

"Well, we can at least help move his car somewhere safe and sort him out a taxi," said his wife. "He needs our help."

So the husband got out of bed again, got dressed, and went downstairs. He opened the door, but couldn't to see the stranger anywhere so he shouted, "Hey, do you still want a push?"

In answer, he heard a voice call out, "Yes please!"

So, still unable to see the stranger, he shouted, "Where are you?"

"I'm over here, mate," the stranger replied, "on your swing."

The president of the Worcester Vegetarian Society couldn't control himself any more. He simply had to try some pork, just to see what it tasted like. So one day he told his members he was going away for a short break. He left town and headed to the restaurant at The Bank House Country Club. He sat down, ordered a roasted pig, and waited impatiently for his treat. After a while, he heard someone call his name, and, to his horror, he saw one of his members walking towards him. At exactly the same moment, the waiter arrived at his table, with a huge platter, holding a whole roasted pig with an apple in its mouth. "Isn't this place something?" said the president, thinking quickly, "Look at the way they serve apples!"

Phil's nephew came to him with a problem. "I have my choice of two women." he said, with a worried frown, "A beautiful, penniless young girl whom I love dearly, and a rich widow who I don't really love."

"Follow your heart," Phil counselled, "marry the girl you love."

"Very well, Uncle Phil," said the nephew, "that's sound advice. Thank you."

"You're welcome." replied Phil with a smile, "By the way, where does the widow live?"

At a doctor's surgery in Tenbury Wells a patient was confiding in his G.P.

"Doctor, last night I made a Freudian slip. I was having dinner with my mother-in-law and wanted to say, 'Could you please pass the butter, ma.' But instead I said, "You silly old cow, you've completely ruined my life and I can't stand the sight of your ugly fizzog.'"

A man walks into a bar in Bromsgrove with a roll of tarmac under his arm and says, "Pint please, and one for the road."

A passenger in a taxi tapped the driver on the shoulder to ask him something.

The driver screamed, lost control of the cab, nearly hit a bus, drove up over the curb and stopped just inches from a large plate glass window.

For a few moments everything was silent in the cab, then the driver said, "Please, don't ever do that again. You scared the daylights out of me."

The passenger, who was also frightened, apologised and said he didn't realise that a tap on the shoulder could frighten him so much, to which the driver replied, "I'm sorry, it's really not your fault at all. Today is my first day driving a cab. I've been driving a hearse for the last twenty-five years."

WORCESTERSHIRE Wit & Humour

A high-rise building was going up in Worcester and three steel erectors sat on a girder having their lunch.

"Oh, no, not cheese and pickle again," said Jim, the first one, "if I get the same again tomorrow, I'll jump off the girder."

Harry opened his packet. "Oh, no, not a chicken salad with mayo and lettuce on granary," he said. "if I get the same again tomorrow, I'll jump off too."

Owen, the third man, opened his lunch. "Oh, no, not another potato sandwich," he said. "if I get the same again tomorrow, I'll follow you two off the girder."

The next day, Jim got cheese and pickle. Without delay, he jumped. Harry saw he had chicken salad with mayo and lettuce on granary, and with a wild cry, he leapt too. Then the third man,

WORCESTERSHIRE Wit & Humour

Owen, opened his lunchbox. "Oh, no," he said. "potato sandwiches." And he too jumped.

The foreman, who had overheard their conversation, reported what had happened, and the funerals were held together.

"If only I'd known." sobbed Jim's wife.

"If only he'd said." wailed Harry's wife.

"I don't understand it at all," said Owen's wife. "he always got his own sandwiches ready."

At a school in Kempsey, the maths teacher poses a question to little Lee, "If I give £500 to your dad on 12% interest per annum, what will I get back after two years."

"Nothing." says Lee.

"I am afraid you know nothing about maths, Lee," says the teacher crossly.

"I'm afraid too, sir," replies Lee, "you don't know nothing about me dad."

A pupil at a school in Tenbury Wells asked his teacher, "Are 'trousers' singular or plural?"

The teacher replied, "They're singular on top and plural on the bottom."

A farmer from Market Drayton in Shropshire once visited a farmer based near Wickhamford in Worcestershire. The visitor asked, "How big is your farm?"

The Worcestershire farmer replied, "Can you see those trees over there? That's the boundary of my farmland."

"Is that all?" said the Shropshire farmer, "It takes me three days to drive to the boundary of my farm."

The Wickhamford man looked at him and said, "I had a car like that once."

The nervous young batsman playing for the Stone Cricket Club was having a very bad day. In a quiet moment in the game, he muttered to the one of his team mates, "Well, I suppose you've seen worse players."

There was no response…so he said it again. "I said 'I guess you've seen worse players'."

His team mate looked at him and answered, "I heard you the first time. I was just trying to think…"

In The Red Lion at Stifford's Bridge a newcomer asked a local man, "Have you lived here all your life?"

The old man took a sip of his ale and, after a long pause, replied, "Don't know yet!"

A young actor is very excited about appearing at the Palace Theatre in Redditch and can't wait to tell his father.

"Dad, guess what? I've just got my first part in a play. I play the role of a man who's been married for thirty years."

"Well, keep at it, son," replies his father, "Maybe one day you'll get a speaking part."

Q: What do you do when a Telford United fan throws a pin at you?
A: Run like mad, he's got a grenade in his mouth.

A man goes to his G.P. in Hagley and says, "Doc, I can't stop singing *The Green Green Grass of Home*."

The doctor says, "That sounds like Tom Jones syndrome."

"Is it common?" asks the man.

"It's not unusual." the doctor replies.

Q: What do you call a ghost that likes curries?
A: A baltigiest

A man rushed into the Kidderminster Hospital and asked a nurse for a cure for hiccups. Grabbing a cup of water, the nurse quickly splashed it into the man's face.

"What did you that for?" screamed the man, wiping his face.

"Well, you don't have the hiccups now, do you?" said the nurse.

"No." replied the man. "But my wife out in the car does."

A woman from Bewdley called Brenda was still not married at thirty-five and she was getting really tired of going to family weddings especially because her old Aunt Maud always came over and said, "You're next!"

It made Brenda so annoyed, she racked her brains to figure out how to get Aunt Maud to stop.

Sadly, an old uncle died and there was a big family funeral. Brenda spotted Aunt Maud in the crematorium, walked over, pointed at the coffin and said, with a big smile, "You're next!"

A man was waiting for his meal in a Chinese restaurant in Worcester when a duck waddled up to him holding a red rose. The duck says, "Your eyes sparkle like diamonds, my sweet love." "Waiter," shouted the diner, "I asked for a-ROMATIC duck."

Many years ago there was a dispute between two villages, one in Worcestershire and the other in Shropshire. One day the villagers heard the cry, "One man from Worcestershire is stronger than one hundred Shropshire men."

The villagers in Shropshire were furious and immediately sent their hundred strongest men to engage with the enemy. They listened, horrified by the screams and shouts. After hours of fighting, all was quiet but none of the men returned.
Later on, the same voice shouted out, "Is that the best you can do?"

This fired up the people from Shropshire and they rallied round, getting a thousand men to do battle. After days of the most frightful blood-curdling sounds, one man emerged from the battlefield, barely able to speak, but with his last breath he managed to murmur, "It's a trap, there's two of them!"

Peter walked up to the sales lady in the clothing department of a large store in Redditch.

"I would like to buy my wife a pretty pair of tights," he said. "Something cute with love-hearts or flower patterns."

"Oh, that's so sweet," exclaimed the sales lady, "I'll bet she'll be really surprised."

"I'll say," said Peter, "she's expecting a new diamond ring!"

A man and his wife walked past a swanky new restaurant in Great Malvern. "Did you smell that food?" the woman asked. "Wonderful!"

Being the kind-hearted, generous man that he was, her husband thought, "What the heck, I'll treat her!"

So they walked past it a second time.

One day at the Worcester Royal Hospital, a group of primary school children were being given a tour. A nurse showed them the x-ray machines and asked them if they had ever broken a bone.

One little boy raised his hand, "I did!"

"Did it hurt?" the nurse asked.

"No!" he replied.

"Wow, you must be a very brave boy!" said the nurse. "What did you break?"

"My sister's arm!"

Did you hear about the truck driver from Shrewsbury who was seen desperately chiselling away at the brickwork after his lorry became stuck at the entrance to a tunnel?

"Why don't you let some air out of your tyres?" asked a helpful passer-by.

"No, mate," replied the driver, "it's the roof that won't go under, not the wheels."

Did you hear about the last wish of the henpecked husband of a house-proud wife?

He asked to have his ashes scattered on the carpet.

Pete and Larry hadn't seen each other in many years. They were having a long chat, telling each other all about their lives. Finally Pete invited Larry to visit him in his new flat in Worcester. "I have a wife and three kids and I'd love to have you visit us."

"Great. Where do you live?"

"Here's the address. There's plenty of parking behind the flat. Park and come around to the front door, kick it open with your foot, go to the lift and press the button with your left elbow, then enter! When you reach the sixth floor, go down the hall until you see my name on the door. Then press the doorbell with your right elbow and I'll let you in."

"Great. But tell me...what is all this business of kicking the front door open, then pressing buttons with my right, then my left elbow?"

Pete answered, "Surely you're not coming empty-handed?"

Many years ago, a miner fell down pit-shaft at Beech Tree Colliery in Foxcote.

The deputy shouted, "Have you broken anything, lad?"

"No," called back the miner, "there's not much to break down here!"

Did you hear about the fight in the chip shop last week?
Six fish got battered!

There were two fish in a tank, one says, "You man the guns, I'll drive."

A man's car stalls on a country road near the Wyre Forest. When he gets out to fix it, a horse in the nearby field comes up alongside the fence and leans over.

"Your trouble is probably with the injectors," says the horse.

Startled, the man jumps back and runs down the road until he meets a farmer. He tells the farmer his story.

"Was it a large white horse with a black mark over the right eye?" asks the farmer.

"Yes, yes." the agitated man replies.

"Oh, I wouldn't listen to her," says the farmer, "she doesn't know anything about cars."

One day a Shropshire boy was playing in the back garden when he suddenly shouted.

"Mum, why is my Ludlow Town top lying on the grass?"

His Mum looked out the window and shouted, "The thieving gits stole my pegs!"

"You're looking glum," the captain of Barnt Green C.C. remarked to one of his players.

"Yes, the doctor says I can't play cricket." said the downcast man.

"Really?" replied the captain, "I didn't know he'd ever seen you play?"

When the manager of Telford United started to tell the team about tactics, half the players thought he was talking about a new kind of peppermint.